REMINDERS FOR HEALING

A Little Book of Comfort for Challenging Times

Sheridan Hill

REMINDERS FOR HEALING

A Little Book of Comfort for Challenging Times

Sheridan Hill

Reali Life Stories, LLC

Reminders for Healing

A Little Book of Comfort for Challenging Times
Copyright © July 2016 by Sheridan Hill

All rights reserved. No part of this publication may be reproduced, distributed, or transmitted in any form or by any means, including photocopying, recording, or other electronic or mechanical methods, without the prior written permission of the publisher, except in the case of brief quotations embodied in critical reviews and certain other noncommercial uses permitted by copyright law. For permission requests, write to the publisher at the address below:

Real Life Stories, LLC
PO Box 248
Montreat, NC 28757

Ordering Information: Special discounts are available on quantity purchases. For details, contact the publisher at the address above or call: 828-785-2828 or see the shopping cart page of ReaLifeStories.com.
Printed in the United States of America

Cover photo by: Patrick J. Considine

Library of Congress Control Number: 2016914171
Publisher's Cataloging-in-Publication data:
Hill, Sheridan

Reminders for Healing: A Little Book of Comfort for Challenging Times / Sheridan Hill. 35 pages.

ISBN 10 : 0-9905087-3-0
ISBN 13: 978-0-9905087-3-1

1. Bereavement. Self-Help. Death. Grief. Inspirational.

Real Life Stories, LLC, First printing July 2016

For everyone who has experienced loss

Photo courtesy of Sean Considine

Coming into grief

is like receiving a frog

from the hands of an

excited child.

You do not really want it,

you don't know what to do with it,

and you don't know how to give it back.

Photo courtesy of Rebecca D'Angelo

Your old ways and habits

may soothe you

or they may no longer serve you.

Grief is scary because

it calls us to change.

Trust that something good is coming.

Photo courtesy of Rebecca D'Angelo

Loss leaves a hole

in the center of your life.

Try not to fill that hole

too quickly.

Can you be with the emptiness

just as you might

sit with a sick friend?

Photo by Sheridan Hill

∿

When the pain is there,

the first thing you must do

is dig down deep

to find compassion

for yourself.

Enter into compassion.

Evoke compassion.

Photo courtesy of Catalina Considine

When the pain comes,

let it out.

Say it.

Sing it.

Dance it.

Drum it.

Release it into the sunshine.

It might be the start

of something beautiful.

Sometimes you will hear laughter

—yours, or someone else's—

and the echoes of laughter

will seem strange.

Allow yourself to enjoy that sound.

Photo courtesy of Desigva Design

When my mother became very sick, she said, "I don't want to die now; I've just gotten my apartment fixed the way I like it!"

Photo courtesy of Patrick J. Considine

Sometimes, the sense of loss

is so strong

I am embarrassed.

I don't want anyone to know

how much it hurts.

Then I remember:

everyone alive

has known pain.

Photo courtesy of Rebecca D'Angelo

Grief is like

The storm before the rainbow.

First, there are dark skies,

terrible thunder

and fiery bolts of lightning.

Then, if you know where to look,

there is peace

and heavenly beauty.

Believe in the storm.

Believe in the rainbow.

∼

The first time I let myself feel grief

I thought my body would break

from the force of it.

Then the break became

a furnace burning.

In time, it became an opening

where joy pours in.

Photo courtesy of Danny Hashimoto

Let joy pour in.

Photo courtesy of Sean Considine

I have prayed for deliverance.

I have tried to give thanks

for this moment.

Thank you for this life.

Thank you for this pain.

Thank you for this joy.

Photo courtesy of Danny Hashimoto

It is not easy to find gratitude

when you are in pain.

Try it, when you can.

Gratitude turns hard times

into butterflies.

Photo courtesy of Sean Considine

∼

When loss comes,

Be gentle with yourself.

Be an understanding parent

towards the part of you

that hurts.

Photo courtesy of Danny Hashimoto

When your world seems to be changing,

avoid everything seductive.

Go for a walk.

Try an exercise class.

See a movie or a concert.

Call a friend.

Take a nap.

Go to the playground and swing.

∽

One day in the hammock
My grandson said to me,
"Nanna, I think you will
die before I will."
"You can still talk to me
when I'm dead," I told him,
my eyes wet.
"How?" he asked, his eyes big.
"Love is stronger than death,"
I said.

Photo courtesy of Rebecca D'Angelo

Grief can be a leak

in your inner reservoir.

Drink deeply

from what nourishes your inner life.

Replenish your soul.

A Mourner's Bill of Rights and Responsibilities

It is my firm conviction that the forces of love always accompany the forceful emotions of grief. That love is here to support us in our grief—always—and that we must not let the violence of grief separate us from love. From our own inner light.

It takes a strong heart and a determined mind, working together, to rein in your thoughts from the depths of grief. But failing to do so means you are missing the whole point of the dreaded loss.

When loss comes, it creates a hole. As Martin Prechtel says, be sure to plant something good in that hole.

I created *A Mourner's Bill of Rights and Responsibilities* to remind myself that we who mourn deserve the right to grieve in our own unique fashion, and we also are given sacred responsibilities. Among those are the honest exploration of how grief is moving in our lives and the responsibility to educate others about our grief process.

More than anything, we who mourn have the responsibility to learn to love life again with more passion than ever.

It is my prayer that these words bring you hope, again and again.

Sheridan Hill

A Mourner's Bill of Rights and Responsibilities

© 2015 Sheridan Hill

 I have the right to be sad, and to be angry (including at the Divine), and the responsibility to not hurt myself or others.

 I have the right to be in shock, fear, denial, and the responsibility to move through it organically, in my own time.

 I have the right to weep, and the responsibility to acknowledge my tears.

 I have the right to express my grief, and the responsibility to find those who can allow me to express it.

 I have the right to protest the injustice of my loss, and the responsibility to be a loving parent towards my body, mind, and soul.

I have the right to mourn all of my losses, regardless of how supposedly small, how global, how old, how invisible, or how un-nameable, and I have the responsibility to articulate my grief.

I have the right to be free of my pain, and the responsibility to mourn for as long as it takes.

I have the right to move in and out of mourning over days, months, and years, and I have the responsibility to educate others about my grief process.

I have the right to heal, and the responsibility to ask for what I need to transform my suffering.

I have the right to laugh, to be joyful, to fall in love with life again, and the responsibility to renew my capacity for love.

www.griefcircle.net

Sheridan Hill as a child with her mother, Troyanne Ross

The Grief and Forgiveness Circle

In January, 2016, Sheridan Hill founded the Grief and Forgiveness Circle in Black Mountain, North Carolina.

Open to all, the Grief and Forgiveness Circle meets in the spirit of inquiry. We use creative discussion, brief readings, and simple activities to witness what grief is and how it moves in us, find what helps, what is not helpful. We work with related topics, including how to forgive and freedom from fear.

In the spirit of Francis Weller's work, we acknowledge that, "There is some strange intimacy between grief and aliveness, some sacred exchange between what seems unbearable and what is most exquisitely alive." One of our resources is Francis Weller's book, "The Wild Edge of Sorrow."

In the spirit of Martin Prechtel's work, we acknowledge that, "Grief expressed out loud for someone we have lost, or a country or home we have lost, is in itself the greatest praise we could ever give them. Grief is praise, because it is the natural way love honors what it misses." Sometimes, we read from Prechtel's book, "The Smell of Rain on Dust: Grief and Praise."

Guidelines for Creating Safety and Intimacy in our circle

We meet in circle to explore grief and to bear silent, compassionate witness to mourning.

We invite healing, but this is not a therapy group.

We meet for one hour.

This is a confidential group: what is said here stays here.

We understand it is important not to offer praise, nor judgment, nor what we might think is "helpful" advice, to another.

We will not compare one loss to another; all losses are utterly unique.

We will remember to relax and breathe deeply in this circle and to invite healing

About the Author

Author Sheridan Hill claims the title of Master Griever. Her grief work is informed by workshops with Sobonfu Some, Frances Weller, and Robert Sardello, Ph.D. as well as their books, and the writings of Martin Prechtel and Maladoma Some. Hill first confronted grief as a teenager when she lost a parent tragically. She served for nearly three years as a volunteer for a nonprofit hospice, singing and playing the harp at the bedside of hospice patients.

"My own life, and my work as a biographer, have led me to conclude that there is a whopping backlog of ungrieved losses packed inside everyone; the sooner we set about this work, the better. And, we need to help each other through it."

Hill facilitates the Grief and Forgiveness Circle in Black Mountain, North Carolina and posts to the website www.griefcircle.net. Copies of this book may be purchased from the shopping cart page of www.ReaLifeStories.com.

www.ingramcontent.com/pod-product-compliance
Lightning Source LLC
Chambersburg PA
CBHW041744040426
42444CB00001B/18